Scottish
First Names

SCOTTISH FIRST NAMES

George Mackay

Lomond

© 1998 Waverley Books Ltd
David Dale House
New Lanark ML11 9DJ

ISBN 0 947782 43 5

Printed and bound by Mackays of Chatham

2 4 6 8 10 9 7 5 3 1

Contents

Introduction

This book provides a guide to the range of Scottish names that can be given to babies and gives the origins and meaning of those names. It also lists the names in most common use in Scotland, whether Scottish or not.

Scotland through much of the twentieth century was much more conservative in choosing children's names than England, the USA or Australia. In most families, the same names were passed on from one generation to the next. This has now changed completely, and names are given because the parents like the sound or the associations. Very few of the current top ten names for girls or boys were in the top ten even twenty years ago. But many of today's most popular names are shortened forms of the older names. And names at present felt to be old-fashioned as first names are still very often used as middle names and may yet return to favour.

Nowadays, there are three main trends in naming children – one that refers back to Scottish history and looks for traditional Scottish or Gaelic names; a second that is influenced by the mass media, especially television, common to the English-speaking world; and the third is the way in which so many 'pet' forms of names, like Katie or Ben, have become proper names in their own right, a sign of a new, less formal approach to naming. A fourth trend is steadily developing with girls' names – the combined name, like Beth-Anne or Emma-Jane. The fashion in names is likely to remain changeable.

As the focus of this book is on Scottish names, the selection has been made according to the following guidelines:

1. Names that are Scottish in origin and were originally only used in Scotland or by families of Scottish descent (like Angus, Duncan, Morag, Torquil).
2. Names that are used by the whole English-speaking world, but that are either more popular in Scotland than anywhere else, like Alison and, until recently, James and Alexander; or have a special significance to Scotland because of some historical link, like Robert, John, David. This includes names like Clyde, which have been re-imported to Scotland as first names from the former colonies.
3. Gaelic names – a range of names once restricted to Gaelic-speaking Scotland but which are nowadays often considered or chosen by non-Gaelic-speaking families.
4. Names that are not specially Scottish but are currently very popular in Scotland, like Emma, Jade or Mark.

Names in groups 1, 2 and 3 are given a * to distinguish them. Names are arranged from A to Z, apart from the Gaelic names, which are listed separately at the end. But some Gaelic names already in general use, like Alastair and Mhairi, are in the main list.

In earlier generations, a typically Scottish practice was to give a boy his mother's surname as his first name. This is much less common now, but may be part of the reason why so many surnames have also come into use as first names, like Cameron, Campbell, Ross.

Another Scottish tradition was to give a girl her father's name, simply adding -ina to the end. Particularly common once in the Highlands and Islands, where Hughinas and Duncaninas were to be found, it is now a rare practice.

With each name, the origin, meaning, pet forms and alternative forms are given. When giving a child a name, parents should remember that there is a law of social behaviour, that when a name can be shortened, it will be shortened. Make sure you like the short form too. Where relevant, a name's historical or particular Scottish connection is pointed out. There is a pronunciation guide for the Gaelic names.

The Changing First Names of Scotland

1935

Boys		Girls	
1.	John	1.	Margaret
2.	James	2.	Mary
3.	William	3.	Elizabeth
4.	Robert	4.	Catherine
5.	Alexander	5.	Annie
6.	George	6.	Isabella
7.	Thomas	7.	Agnes
8	David	8.	Jean
9.	Andrew	9.	Helen
10.	Ian	10.	Janet

1958

1.	John	1.	Margaret
2.	James	2.	Ann(e)
3.	William	3.	Elizabeth
4.	David	4.	Linda
5.	Robert	5.	Mary
6.	Ian	6.	Catherine

7.	Thomas	7.	Carol(e)
8.	Alan	8.	Susan
9.	Alexander	9.	Helen
10.	Brian	10.	Fiona

1996

1.	Ryan	1.	Emma
2.	Andrew	2.	Amy
3.	Liam	3.	Lauren
4.	Jack	4.	Shannon
5.	Connor	5.	Rebecca
6.	Scott	6.	Chloe
7.	James	7.	Megan
8.	Daniel	8.	Sarah
9.	Ross	9.	Hannah
10.	Jordan	10.	Rachel

Names A–Z

A

Aaron
From Hebrew root words meaning 'great height'. A Biblical name: Aaron was brother of Moses, but it was not much used until recently. Over two hundred Aarons were named in 1996.

Abbie, Abigail
From Hebrew, 'handmaiden'. The pet form Abbie is more frequent now than the original, although both are popular. Pet forms include Gail.

Adam
From a Hebrew root word meaning 'man', the name of the first man as recorded in the Bible. Always a popular name, recorded from the thirteenth century. Adam Smith (1723–90) was the founder of modern political economy.

*Adamnan
From Gaelic Adhamhnan (Yow-nan). Either from a pet form of Adam, or from the Old Gaelic word *omun*, 'fear, terror'. Adamnan, abbot of the monastery of Iona (seventh century) wrote the life story of St Columba.

Aeneas

From Greek, *aineias*, 'praise'. A popular name in past times. Aeneas was one of the heroes of the Trojan War, celebrated in Virgil's *Aeneid* as the founder of Rome. It was once wrongly connected with the similar-sounding Angus. Aeneas Macdonnell of Glengarry was an ace fighter pilot in the Battle of Britain.

*Agnes

From Greek *agneia*, 'pure, chaste'. St Agnes was an early Christian martyr. This was once a very common name in Scotland, seventh in popularity in 1935, although not currently in vogue. Pet forms include Aggie, Nancy. Agnes Dunbar, 'Black Agnes' (*c.*1312–69) held Dunbar Castle against the invading English.

*Aidan✓

A pet form of the Gaelic name Aed, meaning 'fire, fiery one', with the diminutive -an added. Aidan was king of Dalriada (sixth/seventh century), and St Aidan was a seventh-century bishop of Lindisfarne.

*Aiken

A pet form of Adam, shortened to Ad, with -kin added. Aiken Drum is the 'hero' of an old nursery song.

*Aileen

An English form of Gaelic Eibhlin, Helen. *See also* Eileen, Helen.

*Ailsa

Ailsa Craig is the rock that rises off the Ayrshire coast, from the Norse Aelsi, 'Aela's isle'. It makes an attractive name for a girl, helped by its seeming to be a Scottish form of Elsie.

Aimee *see* Amy.

Aimil *see* Emily.

*Alan, Allan

Traced both from old Gaelic Ailene ('rock-like'), and Norman French Alain, perhaps from Alemannus, the German tribal name. A popular name since the time of the early Stewarts, when Alan FitzWalter, High Steward of Scotland, first took that surname. The form Allen is infrequent in Scotland. Allan Ramsay (1684–1758), the poet, was father of Allan Ramsay (1713–84), the portrait painter.

Alana

A feminine form of Alan, in fairly regular use. The form Alanna is Irish, from Gaelic *a leanbh*, 'o child'.

*Alastair, Alistair, Alister

From Alasdair, the Gaelic form of Alexander. Pet forms are Al, Aly. Alistair Blair is a leading fashion designer, Ali Bain a celebrated fiddle-player.

*Alban √

From Gaelic Alba, Scotland. A name that proclaims its owner as a Scotsman. *See also* Scott.

*Alec, Alex, Alick

Shortened forms of Alexander, sometimes used as names in their own right. Sir Alec Douglas-Home was Prime Minister of Britain; Alex Ferguson is a notable football manager.

*Alexander

Greek, Alexander, 'defender of men'. A name popular throughout Europe, in memory of Alexander the Great (c.360–330 BC). Introduced to Scotland from Hungary by Queen Margaret, wife of King Malcolm Canmore, it was the name of three Scots kings. It became so popular in Scotland that its pet form, Sandy, is a synonym for a Scot. Among many famous bearers is Alexander Graham Bell (1847–92), inventor of the telephone.

Alexandra

Female version of Alexander. Pet forms are Alex, Sandi, Sandy. *See* Sandra. Also found as Alexandria, although this is really a place name.

Alice

From Old German *adel*, 'noble'. It has long been in limited use in Scotland, although Lewis Carroll's tales gave it more currency in the nineteenth and twentieth centuries. An alternative form is Alicia. *See also* Alison.

Alick *see* Alec.

*Alison

A form of Alice, very often used in Scotland. It is sometimes spelt Alyson or Allison. Alison Cockburn wrote a version of 'The Flowers of the Forest'.

Alistair, Alister *see* **Alastair.**

Alan *see* **Alan.**

Allison *see* **Alison.**

*Alpin
Of uncertain origin, probably Pictish. A name of Pictish kings as well as of the father of Kenneth MacAlpin, first king of the Picts and Scots. In the nineteenth century it was popularised by Scott ('These are Clan Alpin's warriors true . . .').

Alyson *see* **Alison.**

Amanda
From Latin *amanda*, 'deserving love': a popular name in the 1980s. Pet form is Mandy.

Amy
From French *aimée*, 'beloved one'. One of the most popular girls' names, second in 1996. The form Aimee is also much used.

Andrea *see* **Andrina.**

*Andrew, Andro
From Greek Aindreas, 'manly'. The name of the apostle Andrew, patron saint of Scotland, and so a very frequently chosen boy's name throughout the centuries and the second most common in 1996. The pet form is Andy. Sir Andrew Wood (1460–1540) was a Scottish naval commander.

*Andrina

A still used form of Andrewina, the feminine form of
Andrew. Andrea is more often found today.

Andro *see* Andrew.

*Angus

From Gaelic Aonghas, meaning 'the unique one, the only
choice'. It may be Pictish in origin, certainly it is a name
that goes back to before the eighth century. A Pictish king
Angus died in AD 761.

Ann, Anne, Anna

From a Hebrew root word meaning 'grace', these names
are cognate with Hannah, mother of the prophet Samuel,
and St Anne, mother of the Virgin Mary. Pet forms include
Annie, Nanna, Nannie. Annie Lennox is a celebrated pop/
soul singer.

Annabel, Annabella

Either from the fusion of Anna and *bella*, 'beautiful', or a
variant of Amabel, from Latin *amabilis*, 'lovable'.

Annette

French for 'little Ann'. This diminutive has long been a
name in its own right.

Archibald

From Old English Arcenbald, a name meaning perhaps
'bold and true'. A popular name in Scotland, especially
among the Campbells. Archibald Sturrock (1835–93) was
a notable locomotive designer.

Arabella
From Latin *orabilis*, 'prayer-worthy'. An old-established name, although never widely used.

Arthur
A name redolent of Celtic legend in the stories of King Arthur and the Round Table. From Greek *arctos*, 'bear', through Celtic art. The source of the name has also been suggested as the old Gaelic root *ar-* 'plough'. In the far north, it may originally have been a form of the Scandinavian name Ottar. Sir Arthur Conan Doyle (1859–1930) was the creator of Sherlock Holmes.

Ashley, Ashleigh
From an Old English root meaning 'ash wood', these are old surnames that have sprung up of recent years as girls' first names, often used in combination, as in Ashley-Anne. Both forms are very popular, with Ashley in the lead.

*Athol, Atholl
From the district in Perthshire and used mostly by those with a connection there. From Gaelic Fotla, one of the seven sons of the legendary Pictish king Cruithne. A boy's name, sometimes also spelt Athole.

*Aulay
In occasional use, especially with the surname Macaulay. A boy's name, from the Gaelic personal name Amalghaidh, a form of the Scandinavian name Olaf.

B

Barry
Also spelt Barrie, especially in Angus where the name originates from the place name Barry (named after a Norman immigrant of the fourteenth century). An alternative derivation is Gaelic *bearrach*, 'spear'. St Barry was an early Celtic missionary in Scotland.

Bella
A shortened form of Isabella or Annabella, or Christabel. Often a pet name in the past and occasionally used as a first name in its own right, although currently deemed old-fashioned.

Ben, Benjamin
From Hebrew, 'favourite son'. A Biblical name; Benjamin was the youngest son of Jacob. The pet form Ben is used far more often than the full form. Other pet forms are Benny, Benjie.

Bertram
From Old English Beorhtram, 'shining raven'. Uncommon; its shortened forms Bertie or Bert are also used.

Beth, *Betha
Shortened forms of Elizabeth, but Beth has overtaken the

original. Betha may also be derived in its own right from Gaelic *beatha*, 'life'.

Betsy, Betty *see* **Elizabeth.**

Biddy *see* **Bridget.**

Bill, Billy
Shortened forms of William. Billy Bremner was one of the great footballers of the 1960s and 1970s.

*Blair
A surname, increasingly often found as a boy's first name. Originally a location name from the numerous places called Blair, Gaelic, meaning 'a level field'.

Bob, Bobby *see* **Robert.**

Bonnie
An import from North America, although originally from Scots *bonnie*, 'beautiful', brought from Scotland to the USA, where it was first used as a name, including that of the notorious girl gangster Bonnie Parker. *See also* Clyde.

Brandon, Brendan
A Scots-Irish name, perhaps from Old Gaelic *bran*, 'raven'; after the energetic Celtic saint who travelled the Hebridean seas, and perhaps the Atlantic, in a coracle. Brandon is the form more often used.

*Brenda
Sometimes taken to be a feminine form of Brendan but

more likely separately derived from Scandinavian *brandr*, 'sword', as it was common in the Northern Isles. Brenda Blethyn is a well-known actress.

Brendan *see* Brandon.

Brian
A Celtic name brought by the Bretons who accompanied the Normans, from the root word *bri*, 'dignity'; recorded in Scotland from the twelfth century.

Bridget
The name of a great Celtic saint (*c*.452–523), and prior to that a pagan goddess. More common in Ireland than in Scotland; here it is also found as Brigid. The French form Brigitte was made popular for a time by the actress Brigitte Bardot. Shortened forms are Bridie and Biddy.

Bridie *see* Bridget.

*Bruce
Originally a surname, from Norman French de Brix (a place name in Normandy). This became de Brus and then Bruce. The first Bruce came to Scotland in the reign of David I and became lord of Annandale. But it is the great name of Robert Bruce (1274–1329), the king who regained Scotland's independence, that is remembered. As a first name it goes back to the eighteenth century. It became very popular in Australia and is still thought of as the typical name of an Australian male. Perhaps as a result it is now little used in Scotland.

C

Caitlin

From Irish Gaelic, English Kathleen. At present this is the most popular of the numerous forms of Catherine.

*Callum, Calum

Forms of Malcolm, now more often used than the original.

*Cameron

A surname from both Highland (Gaelic *cam-sron*, 'hook nose', a famous clan of Lochaber), and Lowland, mainly from the parish of Cameron, formerly Camberone, in Fife. The exploits of the Cameron Highlanders regiment may have helped to give it currency as a first name. Originally a first name by the use-of-mother's-name process, but now very popular in general use. Pet form is Cammie. Sir Cameron Mackintosh is a well-known musical impresario. In the United States it is now used also as a girl's name, for example, the film actress Cameron Diaz.

*Campbell

Surname of the great Argyll clan (Gaelic *cam-beul*, 'wry mouth') but now in general usage as a first name.

Cara

From Latin *cara*, 'dear', although probably a version of Carol; an increasingly popular name.

Carl *see* Charles.

Carly
A shortened form of Charlotte that has become a name in its own right. Carly Simon is a singer and songwriter.

Carol
Feminine form of Charles. A shortened form of Caroline and more often used. Also spelt Carole. Carola is also occasionally used.

Cathella
A combination name of Catherine and Ella or other names ending in -ella.

Catherine, Katherine
From Greek *katharos*, 'pure', the name of an early Christian martyr. Always a popular name in Scotland, although now overtaken by Caitlin and Katie and around fiftieth in popularity. The spelling Katharine is less often found. Pet forms include Kate, Kay, Cath, Cathy. Catherine Glover was the Fair Maid of Perth in Scott's novel of the same name.

*Catriona
Gaelic form of Catherine. Stevenson's romance *Catriona* popularised the name in the late nineteenth century. Pet forms include Trina and Tina.

Chantelle, Chantal
From a French girl's name; the first form is the preferred one in Scotland and it came into the top hundred girls' names in 1996.

Charlene *see* Charlotte.

Charlie
A pet form of Charles and Charlotte.

Charles
A royal name, from Old Germanic *ceorl*, 'man'. Given
European prestige by Charlemagne (Carolus Magnus,
c.742–814), it was used in every European country. In
Scotland it survived the unpopularity of Kings Charles I
and II and was helped by memories of 'Bonnie Prince
Charlie'. Other forms of the name now used here include
Carl, Karl and Gaelic Tearlach.

Charlotte
Feminine form of Charles, from Italian Carlotta. Pet forms
include Chatty, Charlie, Lottie. A rarer feminine form is
Charlene. *See also* Carol.

Chelsea
The name of a London district, given currency by the
daughter of President Clinton of the USA and now in the
top fifty names for girls.

Chloe
From Greek, 'green shoot'. It has shot into popularity and
is one of the top ten girls' names.

Chris
The pet form of Christian, Christabel, Christine and
Christopher.

Chrissie
The pet form of Christine, Christian (girl's name) and Christabel.

Christabel
A combination of Christ(ian) and Latin *bella*, 'beautiful'.

Christian
A name for a boy or a girl, originally a girl's, notably the sister of King Robert I, but made popular for boys also by the success of John Bunyan's *Pilgrim's Progress*. Christian Miller wrote about the pains of growing up as a young girl in an aristocratic Scottish household in her book, *A Scottish Childhood*.

Christine, Christina
Forms of Christian, and once popular names but currently outmoded. The pet form Kirsty is very popular in its own right. Other pet forms are Chris, Chrissie.

Christopher
From Greek, meaning 'Christ-bearer', from the legend of St Christopher. A consistently popular name in recent times. Pet forms are Chris, Kit.

*Ciaran *see* Kieran.

Claire, Clare, Clara
From Latin *clara*, 'clear, pure'. The Claire form is more frequent. Clara is now unusual.

Clyde
A river name, re-imported to Scotland as a first name from the USA, where its most notorious holder was the gangster Clyde Barrow (1909–34). *See also* Bonnie.

*Colin
From Gaelic *cailean*, 'youth', a name strongly associated with the Campbell clan whose chief was MacCailean Mor, 'the great son of Colin'. It is unrelated to the English Colin (a short form of Nicholas). Pet form is Col. Sir Colin Campbell (1792–1863) was a celebrated general.

Colleen
From Gaelic *cailean*, 'girl, maid'. Used in Ireland to refer to any girl but a personal name in Scotland.

*Colum, Columba, Colm
Variants of the name of the great Celtic missionary saint of Iona (521–97); from Latin *columba*, 'a dove'.

Connor, Conor
The first form is far more often used. From Irish Gaelic Conchobar, the king of Ulster in the Deirdre legend. One of the most often used boys' names, fifth in 1996. Pet form is Con.

Cosmo
A rare name for a boy, from Greek *kosmos*, 'order'. Cosmo Gordon Lang (1864–1945), born in Fyvie, became Archbishop of Canterbury.

Courtney
A Norman-French surname that has caught on as a modern girl's name.

*Craig
A surname that has become increasingly popular as a boy's first name. From Gaelic *carraig*, 'a rock'.

D

*Dair
A part of the name Alasdair that has become a name in its own right.

Daisy
A flower name. Once quite frequently given, as the music hall song 'Daisy, Daisy' suggests, it is now fairly rare.

*Dallas
A surname now used also as a first name. It comes from the lands of Dallas in Moray (Gaelic *dail eas*, 'field by the waterfall'), after which the Texas city of Dallas was also named.

Daniel
From Hebrew, 'God has judged'. The popularity of many Old Testament names like Amos and Ebenezer has waned, but this one remains very much in vogue. Pet forms are Dan and Danny. Daniel Boone, the American frontiersman (1734–1820), was of Scottish descent.

Danielle
Feminine form of Daniel, from French, and almost as popular for girls as Daniel is for boys.

Darren
Originally a surname, now popular as a boy's name, helped by television. It is well within the top fifty boys' names.

*David
Two Davids were kings of Scotland, *c*.1080–1153 and 1324–71. The name has always been a popular one. Its origin is from the Bible, the Hebrew King David (Dawidh) being 'the beloved of God'. Pet forms are Dave, Davie and, rarely nowadays, Dauvit. David Balfour is the hero of Stevenson's *Kidnapped*.

Davidina
A female form of David, very common in the eighteenth and nineteenth centuries. Other female forms of David more used nowadays are Davina and Davine.

Dean
Dean is a Scots word meaning 'a steep valley', but this name owes its popularity to the film world and the actor James Dean (1931–55).

Deborah
Name of an Old Testament prophetess, from a Hebrew root meaning 'bee'. Pet forms are Debbie, Debs. The film actress Deborah Kerr was born in Helensburgh.

Declan
From the Celtic St Deaglan. An Irish name that has steady use in Scotland.

*Deirdre

From a Gaelic root word meaning 'sorrowful'. It is a name that has been current since the late nineteenth-century interest in Celtic lore. It is rich in Celtic resonance from the Irish-Scottish legend of Deirdre of the Sorrows, a classic of tragic love.

Demi

A girl's name, from French *demi*, 'half', but popular for its sound and its link with the actress Demi Moore. Two-syllable names ending in a vowel are highly popular.

Dennis

St Denis (Latin Dionysius), patron saint of France, was highly regarded in Scotland, but the name is currently out of fashion despite, or because of, the popularity of the comic character Dennis the Menace. Also spelt Denis. Denis Law was one of football's greatest inside forwards.

Denny

A pet form of Dennis, but it can also be from the surname Denny, which comes from the town of the same name in Stirlingshire.

Derek *see* Derrick.

Dermot *see* Diarmid.

Derrick

From the Gothic/Germanic Theodoric, 'ruler of the people'. Also sometimes spelt Derek. The pet form is Derry.

Diana
The moon goddess of the Romans and a powerful female divinity. It has been a first name since the sixteenth century but was not often used. The popularity of Diana, Princess of Wales (1961–97), however, may increase its use.

*Diarmid, Diarmaid
Diarmaid was a great hero of old Celtic legend, said to be buried in Glen Lonan, Argyll. The name means 'he who reverences God'. It is also spelt Dermot.

*Dod
A Scots shortening of George.

*Dolina
A feminine form of Donald, common in Gaelic-speaking areas in the nineteenth and early twentieth centuries and still in use.

Dolly
A pet form of Donaldina, Dorothy and Doris.

*Donald
For long the second most frequently given name in the Highlands after John, but nowadays little used. From Gaelic Domhnall, from a Celtic root, *dubno* or *dumno*, meaning 'great ruler'. Pet forms include Don, Donnie. Donald Ban (*c.*1033–99) was king of Scotland; Donald Caskie (1902–83) was a Scots minister in Paris and hero of the French Resistance in the Second World War.

*Donaldina

A feminine form of Donald, now rare, given to girls whose father was called Donald. Other forms include Donella, Donalda, Dolina.

Donnie *see* Donald.

Dorothy

From Greek, meaning 'gift of God'. Its pet forms include Dodie, Dot, Dolly. The word doll comes from this name. The form Dorothea is also used. Dorothy Dunnett is a well-known writer of historical novels.

*Dougal, Dugald

From old Gaelic Dubhgall, 'dark stranger', probably applied to Norsemen. Rarely used at present. Pet forms include Doug, Dougie. Sir Dugald Clark invented the two-stroke engine in 1879. Dougal Haston (1940–77) was a leading mountain climber.

*Douglas

Originally a surname taken by Flemish immigrants in the twelfth century from the valley location of the first Douglases in the Borders (Gaelic *dubh glas*, 'dark water'). Pet forms are Doug, Dougie. Douglas Dunn is a modern Scottish poet.

*Drew

Part of the name Andrew, it has become a name in its own right. The Norman name Drogo ('stout, strong') also has the same modern form.

*Duff

From Gaelic *dubh*, 'dark'. An ancient surname that is occasionally also used as a first name.

Dugald *see* Dougal.

*Duncan

From Gaelic Donnchaidh (*donn*, 'brown of hair or skin', and *cath*, 'warrior'): 'brown-haired warrior'. The first king of all Scotland was Duncan (*c*.1001–40). Duncan Macrae (1905–67) was a well-loved actor.

Dylan

From Welsh, 'son of the waves'. A popular boy's name, helped by the singer Bob Dylan and by Dylan of *The Magic Roundabout*.

E

Eck, Ecky
Shortened forms of Alexander.

Edgar
From the old English name Eadgar, 'happy spear'. The first Scots Edgar was probably the king (c.1074–1107). Despite this royal connection, it has never been a common name for Scottish boys.

Eileen *see* **Aileen.**

*Eilidh, Ellie
The Gaelic form of Helen in its English and original form. Both forms are in the top hundred for girls, with Eilidh far in the lead.

Elaine
A French form of Helen that has long been popular in Scotland although now rather out of favour. Elaine C. Smith is a popular Scottish actress.

Elizabeth
A Biblical name, from Hebrew Eliseba, 'oath of God'. Elizabeth was the mother of John the Baptist. The shortened or pet forms Lisa and Beth are far more

commonly used than the full name. Other forms are Betty, Betsy, Liz, Lizzie, Libby. Eliza is almost extinct. *See also* Elspeth. Liz Lochhead is a well-known modern poet.

Ella
A pet form of Eleanor and Isabella or other names ending in -ella, now often used as a name in its own right.

Ellen
A form of Helen. Ellen Douglas is the heroine of Scott's *Lady Of the Lake*.

Ellie *see* Eilidh.

*Elspeth
A Scottish form of Elizabeth, sometimes shortened to Eppie.

Emily
Formerly Emilia, from Latin Aemilia, of the Roman Aemilian clan. Its shortened form, Emma, has far overtaken it, although it remains in the top thirty girls' names. Pet forms are Emmy, Em. A Scots form, Aimil, is rare.

Emma
Currently the favourite name for girls in Scotland. From Old German *irmin*, 'universal', brought to Scotland by Norman settlers in the twelfth century, although it can also be a shortened form of Emily. It is only in recent years, helped by television and film adaptations of Jane Austen's novel *Emma*, that it has leapt to its present height of popularity.

*Eoghan ✓

From the Celtic *eo*, 'yew', this is an ancient name that goes back to tree-worship among the Celtic tribes. *See* Evan, Ewan. The name Eugene has also been related to this name.

Eppie *see* Elspeth.

Erin ✓

From Gaelic Eireann, Ireland, 'the western land'. A girl's name that, like Connor and Declan for boys, shows the strong Irish influence on Scottish names.

Etta *see* Henrietta.

Eugene *see* Eoghan.

Euphemia

The name of an early Christian martyr, from a Greek origin meaning 'fair of speech'. In Scotland it has aristocratic overtones from Euphemia, Countess of Ross, who founded Fortrose Cathedral. Phemie is an old-fashioned pet form, and sometimes Fay is used as a shortened form.

*Evan, Ewan, Ewen, Euan

An English-language form of Gaelic Eoghan. It is also the Welsh form of John. A name associated with the Cameron clan among others: 'Come hither, Evan Cameron, and stand beside my knee . . .'

F

*Farquhar
Gaelic Fearchar, from old Gaelic *ver-car-os*, 'very dear one'.

Fay
From old French *fée*, 'witch, fairy', as in the name Morgan le Fay. It is sometimes used as a shortened form of Euphemia.

*Fenella
The English-language form of Gaelic Fionnaghal, from *fionn*, 'white', and *guala*, 'shoulder'.

*Fergus
A royal name among the ancient Celts and Picts, from a Gaelic root, *ver gustu*, 'the only choice'. Fergus MacErc led the Scots colonists from Dalriada in Ulster to the west of Scotland. Pet forms are Ferg, Fergie. A rarer, more Irish form is Fergal.

Ffyona *see* Fiona.

*Fingal
From Gaelic Fionnghal, 'fair-haired stranger', a name given to the blond Norse invaders. Fingal is one of the great heroes of Celtic mythology.

*Finlay

From Gaelic *fionn*, 'fair, and *laoch*, 'hero': 'fair hero'. A surname that is increasingly found as a first name. Finlay Quaye is a well-known Scots-West Indian singer.

*Fiona

Impeccably Scottish-sounding but a coined name from James Macpherson's poem 'Ossian'. However, the male name Fionn, or Finn, meaning 'fair one', is an ancient one. There are many Gaelic legends about Finn MacCool, the giant. Variants include Ffyona. Ffyona Campbell wrote in the 1990s about her walk round the world.

*Flora

From Latin *flora*, 'flower'. A popular name in the Highlands and in increasing use elsewhere. Flora Macdonald (1722–90) was the Jacobite heroine who helped Prince Charles Edward Stuart flee from Benbecula to Portree.

*Forbes

Originally a surname from the lands of Forbes in Aberdeenshire. It became a first name through the custom of naming a boy after his mother's maiden name. Forbes Masson is a well-known Scottish actor.

*Fraser

Originally a clan surname, from Norman French de Fresel, but in frequent use as a first name. Occasionally spelt Frazer.

G

Gary, Garry

A twentieth-century boy's name that has become popular because of the American film star Gary Cooper, who was named after his home town of Gary, Indiana. The form Garry is sometimes found in Scotland, perhaps because of Glen Garry in both Perthshire and Inverness-shire.

*Gavin

The Scots form of Gawain, the Welsh Gwalchmai of Arthurian legend. The original meaning of the name is 'Hawk of Battle'. Gavin Maxwell (1914–69) wrote *Ring of Bright Water* about his tame otters; Gavin Hastings is one of Scotland's great rugby players and was captain of the national side.

Gemma, Jemma

From Latin *gemma*, 'jewel'. It is still in the top forty girls' names, but Gemma's recent popularity seems to be diminishing while Jemma's goes up.

George

From Greek *georgos*, 'farmer'. A common surname in Scotland, although unusual as a first name until relatively modern times. Pet forms are Geordie, Dod, Doddie. The film *Geordie*, from David Walker's novel, helped to keep

the name popular, but it is now quite low in the top
hundred. George Douglas Brown (1869–1902) wrote *The
House with the Green Shutters* under the pseudonym
George Douglas. George Young captained Scotland in
football forty-eight times.

Georgina
Perhaps because of the succession of King Georges in the
eighteenth century, this -ina name developed outside
Scotland. It is also found in Scotland from that period.
Other forms are Georgiana, Georgia, and the pet names
Georgie and Gina.

Gilbert
From Old German *gisil*, 'pledge' or 'hostage', and *berhta*,
'bright'. The Old French form was Gislebert. Known since
the twelfth century, it was at its most popular in the
seventeenth and eighteenth centuries. Pet forms include
Gib, Gibbie and Gil.

Giles
From Greek *aigidion*, 'young goat'. St Giles's name came
from his goatskin dress. He was patron saint of cripples and
beggars, and Edinburgh's cathedral, now High Kirk, was
dedicated to him. It was once also used as a girl's name. *See*
Gillian.

*Gillespie
From Gaelic Gilleasbuig, 'servant of the bishop'. Originally
the name was given to a junior cleric. This was once a
relatively common Scottish name but is now rare.

Gillian
A feminine form of Giles, although not in frequent use until modern times. In Scotland the initial G is soft. Pet forms include Gill, Gillie.

Gina *see* Georgina.

*Gordon
From the surname, which derives from Gordon (perhaps from Old Gaelic *gor dun*, 'hill fort') in Berwickshire. From there the Gordons moved to Strathbogie. Pet forms are Gord, Gordie. It is a little used name at present. Gordon Jackson, who died in 1996, was a well-loved film and television actor.

Grace
A popular name earlier in the twentieth century; by the 1950s it had fallen out of use (despite Princess Grace of Monaco) and now is rare.

*Graeme, Graham, Grahame
From the surname, which probably derives from Grantham in England, which the Norman de Grahames left to come to settle in Scotland, but may also be from Old English and Scots *gray hame*, 'grey house'. Graeme is the most popular form. Graeme Souness is one of Scotland's many well-known football managers.

*Grant
A surname now often found as a first name. From Old French *grand*, 'tall'.

*Gregor, Grigor

From the old Gaelic word *giric*, 'king's crest', this name was later matched with Latin *gregorius*, 'watchman'. The original Gregor was said to be a son of King Kenneth MacAlpin. The shortened form Greg has also become a name in its own right.

Greta

A shortened form of Margaretta. *See* Margaret.

Grigor *see* Gregor.

*Grizel

A shortened form of Griselda, from an Old German name, meaning 'grey warrior maid'. A well-known name in Scottish history, although now rare and often confused with Grace. Grizel Hume (1665–1746) was a heroine of the Covenanters.

H

Haley *see* **Hayley.**

*Hamish
An English-language form of the Gaelic Seumas, James, but much more common than Seumas.

Hannah
From Hebrew Hanani, 'favoured one'. A Biblical name, Hannah was mother of the prophet Samuel. An uncommon name in the past but currently one of the most popular names for girls. *See also* Ann.

Hattie *see* **Henrietta.**

Hayley
Another of the many two-syllable girls' names ending in a vowel sound that dominate the top thirty or so positions. Originally a surname, meaning 'hay field', it took off in the 1960s with the actress Hayley Mills. It can also be spelled as Haley.

Hazel
A popular example of a plant name being used as a girl's name.

*Heather.

First recorded in the nineteenth century and currently the most frequently used of the flower and plant names for girls.

Hector

From the Trojan hero, a Greek name meaning 'holding fast'. It has been a popular name in warlike Scotland since the Middle Ages. Pet forms are Heck, Heckie. Hector Boece (1465–1536) was a chronicler and historian. Sir Hector Macdonald, 'Fighting Mac' (1853–1903), was a general who rose from the ranks.

Helen

From Greek, 'bright one'. The renown of the name goes back to Helen of Troy and was made popular in Christian times by St Helena, who believed she had found the True Cross. Pet forms are Nell, Nella, Nellie.

Henrietta

Feminine form of Henry. In general usage it is found more often in pet form as Hettie, Hattie or Etta.

Holly, Hollie

One of numerous plant names to come into use for girls in the twentieth century and the most popular if both forms are counted. Holly is the more widely used.

Hugh

Norman French Ugues, from Germanic *ugu*, 'spirit'. It early became popular in Scotland. Pet forms include Hughie and, in the north, Hughock. Hugh Clapperton (1788–1827), with a companion, was the first European to make the crossing of the Sahara Desert. Hughie Gallacher (1903–57) was one of the great centre forwards in football.

I

*Iain, Ian
The Gaelic form of John and still very popular, with Iain slightly more favoured than Ian, particularly in Scotland.

Ina
Originally the termination of other names, like Davina; now found as a name in its own right.

*Innes
A surname occasionally used as a first name. From Gaelic *inis*, 'island', an island-dweller. The surname MacInnes, however, comes from Angus.

*Iona
A modern girl's name, inspired by the renewed fame of St Columba's island. It is from an ancient misspelling of Ioua, perhaps meaning 'island of yews'.

Isabel, Isabella, Ishbel, Isobel
From the Portuguese form of Elizabeth, imported from France and in use at least since the thirteenth century when Robert I's ancestor married Isabel, a descendant of William the Lion, and so established the Bruce claim to the throne. Pet forms include Isie, Bell, Bella. Ishbel is an anglicised version of the Gaelic form Iseabhail. Isabella was

the sixth most popular girl's name in 1935; all are little used at present. Isobel, Countess of Buchan, crowned Robert Bruce king in 1307.

*Isla

A name from the Perthshire river and strath. Isla St-Clair, the singer, has helped to establish it, but it was in use in the nineteenth century. Isla Stewart (1885–1910) was a distinguished London hospital matron.

*Islay

From the island, a boy's name chiefly associated with Clan Campbell.

Isobel *see* Isabel.

*Ivor, Ivar

An old Norse personal name, adapted into Gaelic as Iomhar and found mostly in Argyll and Dumbarton, notably among the Colquhouns.

J

Jack

A shortened form of Jacob, from Latin Jacobus, but also
used as a pet form of John. Today it is a highly popular
name in its own right and is among the top ten for boys,
above both James and John. The pet form is Jackie. Jackie
Stewart is a three-times winner of the world motor racing
championship. The writer Jack House (1906–91) was
known as 'Mr Glasgow'.

Jade

An international modern name from the precious stone,
helped by Mick Jagger's daughter.

Jake, Jaikie

Pet forms of Jack, which itself is a variant of James, from
French Jacques. John Buchan's character 'Wee Jaikie' has
helped to give the name an identity of its own.

*James

From Latin Jacobus. The name of an Apostle and of six
kings of Scotland, it has consistently been a very popular
name and is still in the top ten. Pet forms are Jim, Jimmy.
See Jamie. James Watt (1736–1819) is the best known of
Scotland's many engineers.

Jamesina
A feminine form of James that is now rare.

*Jamie ✓
A shortened form of James that has become a very popular name in its own right, perhaps first in England. Through American use it has also become a girl's name, although much less frequently, the best-known bearer being the film actress Jamie Lee Curtis.

Jan
A pet form of the names Jane, Janet and Janice.

Jane
A feminine form of John, from Latin Johanna. It is frequently confused with Jean. Jane Welsh Carlyle (1801–66), wife of Thomas Carlyle, was a gifted writer.

Janet
A pet form of Jane originally. The popularity of this name has suffered as a result of being regarded as a servant's name and rather old-fashioned, as for example the character Janet in the TV series *Dr Finlay's Casebook*. It shares the pet forms Jan, Jenny, Janie with Jane and Janice.

Janice, Janis
Another feminine version of John. The jazz singer Janis Joplin has given this name a touch of international glamour.

Janie
A pet form of the names Jane, Janet and Janice.

Jason
From a Greek root word meaning 'healer'. Jason is one of the great heroes of Greek mythology, but its current, though waning, popularity stems from its television connections. In 1996, 124 babies were named Jason in Scotland.

*Jean, Jeannie
A feminine form of John, from Old French Jehane. Once one of the most popular girls' names in Scotland, it is now no longer in the top hundred. Jeannie Robertson (1908–75) was a well-known folksinger.

Jemma *see* Gemma.

Jennifer, Jenna
A Celtic name, from Welsh Gwenhwyfar, 'fair and yieldng', an accurate description of Arthur's queen, Guinevere, another form of the same name. The short form Jenna has become a name in its own right. Pet forms include Jenny, Jen.

Jenny
A pet form of the names Jane, Janet, Janice and Jennifer, now often used as name in its own right.

Jess, Jessie
Once a pet form of Janet, and more rarely of Jessica, but very often used as a girl's first name in its own right, especially in the nineteenth and early twentieth centuries. Jessie was the fourteenth most popular girl's name in 1935. Jess is more rarely used as a boy's name, after the Biblical Jesse, father of David.

Jessica ✓

From Hebrew, 'seen by God'. Little used in the past but consistently popular in recent years, it is one of the top fifty girls' names.

Jessie *see* Jess.

Jim, Jimmy

Shortened forms of James, rarely used as names in their own right and overtaken in recent years by the increasing popularity of Jamie. Jimmy Johnstone is one of the great Scottish footballers. Jim Clark (1936–68) won twenty-five Grand Prix motor races.

Jo

A pet form of John, Jonathan and Joseph.

Joan

A shortened form of Johanna. It has declined in popularity in recent decades.

Joanne, Joanna

Forms of Johanna. More frequently given now than Joan, their combined number just puts them in the top fifty girls' names of 1996.

*Jock

A pet form of John that once was and perhaps still is synonymous with 'Scotsman', from old army usage when all Scots soldiers were dubbed Jocks. Jocky Wilson has twice won the world darts championship.

Jodie
A form of Judy or Judith, it is among the top fifty girls' names and is still rising in popularity. The film star Jodie Foster adds to its appeal.

Joe *see* Joseph.

Johann, Johanna
A feminine form of John, never frequently used and now rare.

John
Once the most popular of all boys' names, in Scotland as elsewhere, thanks to the beloved Apostle of Christ. Almost abandoned through overuse, it has come back into the top twenty boys' names in 1996. The Gaelic forms, Iain, Ian, also remain popular. Pet forms include Jock, Johnnie. John Muir (1813–1914) was the founder of ecology.

Johnina
A feminine form of John, now obsolete.

Jonathan
From Hebrew, meaning 'God gives'. The best-known Jonathan in the Bible is the lamented companion of David. Although current in Scotland for many centuries, it has never been widely used. Pet forms are Jon, Jo. Other spellings include Johnathan and Jonothan.

Jordan
From a Hebrew root meaning 'downward-flowing'. The Jordan river was the place of Christ's baptism and the

name has been rarely used in the past. Recently it has grown greatly in popularity. In 1996 it was the tenth most popular name for boys. Its resemblance to Gordon may partly account for this.

Joseph
This Biblical name has never been very widely used in Scotland. From a Hebrew root meaning 'God gives', it includes Joseph, son of Jacob, Joseph, the husband of Mary, and Joseph of Arimathea. Pet forms are Jo (also of John and Jonathan) or Joe.

Joshua, Josh
This Biblical name has enjoyed an upsurge in popularity in recent years. It comes from a Hebrew root meaning 'God is kind'. The Old Testament Joshua was one of the greatest captains of Israel. The pet form Josh is now often used in its own right.

K

Karen
A Danish name, pet form of Katarina, but has been adopted into English. Very popular in the 1950s and 1960s but now outmoded.

Karl *see* Charles.

Kate *see* Katie.

Katharine, Katherine *see* Catherine.

Kathleen
A form of Katherine, from Irish Caitlin, and still a name with Irish overtones. Catriona is a more Scottish form.

*Katie, Kate
For long favourite pet names for Catherine, these are now well established as independent names also, with Katie one of the top twenty.

Kay
Occasionally found as a boy's name, as Kay in John Masefield's story *The Magic Box*. Sir Kay was King Arthur's foster brother in the Round Table legends. But in the great

majority of cases, a girl's name in its own right (sometimes as Kaye) or as a pet form of Katherine or Catherine.

Kayleigh
A recent name, perhaps modelled on the now little used Australian name Kylie (from a word meaning 'boomerang'), but Kayleigh is popular and still increasing in use.

*Keir
A surname from a Stirlingshire locality but also from Gaelic *ciar*, 'dark' (*see* Kieran). Keir Hardie (1856–1915), pioneer Labour politician, actually had James as his first name.

*Keith
A surname from East Lothian and Moray locations, it has now become a popular first name. From an old Celtic word for wood, cognate with Welsh *coed*. It is perhaps more usually found now outside Scotland.

Kelvin
The name of the Glasgow river (from Gaelic *caol*, 'narrow' and *abhainn*, 'river') which is sometimes used as a first name.

Ken *see* Kenneth.

*Kennedy
From the Scots-Irish surname, from Gaelic *ceann eidhigh*, 'ugly head': originally a nickname. A name associated with the southwest.

*Kenneth
From Gaelic *coinneach*, 'handsome'. Kenneth MacAlpin (crowned in 843) was first king of the Picts and Scots. It was a favourite name with the prolific Clan MacKenzie ('sons of Kenneth'). Pet forms are Ken, Kenny. Sir Kenneth Macmillan (1929–92) was a leading choreographer of ballet. Kenny Dalglish is a brilliant footballer and football manager.

Keri *see* Kerry.

*Kerr
From the surname, from Gaelic *ciar*, 'dark-haired or complexioned'.

Kerry
A boy's or girl's name but far more frequent with girls. From Ireland, the place name means 'land of the dark-haired people'. Other forms include Kerri, Keri (the last perhaps linked with the Maori name of the opera singer Kiri Te Kanawa).

*Kevin
From Gaelic *caomhin*, 'born handsome', originally an Irish name, from the Celtic St Kevin but now common in Scotland and elsewhere.

Kieran, *Ciaran
From Gaelic *ciar*, 'dark-haired or complexioned'. Kieran is the Irish form, but much more frequently used, although Ciaran is growing rapidly in popularity.

Kimberley
From an English place name that was also given to the South African town. Originally it was a boy's name given after the Boer War, but since the 1940s has been used only for girls. Now it is one of the top fifty girls' names. The pet form is Kim.

Kirsten
Scandinavian in origin, this is a form of Christian or Christine. It is often shortened to Kirsty.

*Kirsty
This pet form of Christine is well established as a name in its own right; it was fifteenth in popularity in 1996.

*Kyle
From Gaelic *caol*, 'a strait'. The name of numerous locations, but in recent times popular as a boy's name, probably regarded as a male form of Kylie/Kayleigh. In 1996, 387 Kyles were named, making it the twenty-third most popular name for a boy.

L

*Lachlan
From Lochlann, Gaelic for Scandinavia ('loch or fjord land'). The Clan MacLachlan descends from Lachlann, son of Gilpatrick (late thirteenth century). The shortened form is Lachie.

Laura
A feminine version of the Latin name Laurentius. Made famous throughout Europe as the adored one in Petrarch's sonnets (fourteenth century), it has lately been overtaken in popularity by Lauren but remains a popular name.

Lauren
A very frequently used girl's name, third in popularity in 1996. It has no Scottish links but perhaps the resemblance to, or slight difference from, Laura and Lorraine has helped it to become established. It is also a film-star name (Lauren Bacall).

Lee
From Old English *lea*, 'meadow', which became a surname. A recently arrived first name, chiefly for boys, and well within the top fifty boys' names of 1996, although it has also been used for girls.

*Lesley
This has become the feminine form of Leslie. Originally a surname from the lands of Leslie in Aberdeenshire.

*Leslie
Once a girl's name ('Saw ye bonnie Leslie . . .?') but now established as the male form.

Lewis
From Old Germanic Chlodowig, 'famous warrior'. The French form is Louis, but this form, perhaps influenced by the Hebridean island's name, is dominant in Scotland and currently of considerable popularity. Hebridean Lewis is from Scandinavian *ljoth-hus*, 'house of song'. Pet forms are Lew, Lewie.

Liam
An Irish form of William, currently very popular (third in 1996). (*See* Gaelic Uilleam). Liam Neeson, the film actor, and Liam Gallagher, the singer, have helped to make it a top name.

Libby *see* Elizabeth.

Lillias
For long a popular girl's name, although little used at the present time. From Italian Liliana, 'lily'. Pet forms are Lil, Lillie.

*Lindsay
One of the boy/girl names, although more often a girl's name. From the surname Lindsay, which came to Scotland

In the twelfth century, perhaps from Lindsey in England. A variant spelling is Linsay.

Lisa, Liza
Pet forms of Elizabeth that are now used as names in their own right.

Liz, Lizzie *see* Elizabeth.

*Lorn, Lorne
In this form a boy's or girl's name, although there is also the female form Lorna. From the Lorn district of Argyll.

*Lorraine
From the French province. Mary of Lorraine, mother of Mary I of Scotland, was regent of Scotland in the sixteenth century. This name 'arrived' in the 1950s, but the similar-sounding Lauren has taken over.

Lottie *see* Charlotte.

Louis *see* Lewis.

Louise, Louisa
Feminine forms of Louis (Lewis); the first is much preferred. Pet forms are Lou, Lulu. A name that has risen in popularity in the past few years along with other French-sounding names.

Lucy
From Latin *lux*, 'light'. The original name was Lucia, French Lucie. Pet forms or variants include Lucille,

Lucinda, Lucilla, Lu. Lucy Ashton is the heroine of Scott's novel *The Bride of Lammermoor*.

Ludovic

From Latin Ludovicus, Lewis. Ludovic Kennedy is a prolific author and broadcaster.

M

Madge
A shortened form of Marjory.

Maggie *see* **Margaret.**

*Magnus
From Latin *magnus*, 'great', but it arrived in Scotland from
the Norse lands where Magnus was a celebrated earl of
Orkney. Magnus Magnusson is a renowned quizmaster and
broadcaster.

*Maisie
A pet form of Marjory and sometimes also of Mary.

*Malcolm
From Gaelic *maol Caluim*, 'servant of Columba'. Malcolm
was a royal name borne by several kings of the Scots and of
united Scotland. Its popularity has declined in recent years.
Pet forms are Malc, Malkie. The businessman Malcolm
Forbes (1919–90) made the first balloon crossing of
America.

*Malise
From Gaelic *maol-Iosa*, 'servant of Jesus'. An unusual
name, historically associated with the surnames Ruthven
and Graham.

Mamie *see* **Mary.**

Marc *see* **Mark.**

*Margaret
From Greek, meaning 'pearl'. St Margaret, queen of
Scotland (died 1093) was the first of numerous royal
Margarets. In the nineteenth century it was common
enough to be considered the national Scottish female
name, and it was the most popular name right through the
first half of the twentieth century. It is, however, little used
today. Megan has left it far behind. It has numerous pet
forms, including Maggie (now outmoded), Meg and Peggy.
Margaret McMillan (1860–1931) was an educational
reformer.

Margo
A shortened form of Margaret, from French Margot.

Marguerite
French form of Margaret, also a flower name.

Marian *see* **Marion.**

Marie *see* **Mary.**

Marion, Marian
From a fusion of the Biblical names Mary and Ann. But in
the nineteenth and early twentieth centuries, Marion was
also used for boys. The American film star John Wayne
(1907–79) was originally Marion Michael Morrison of
Scots descent.

*Marjorie

From French Marguerite (Margaret). A royal name from
the thirteenth century. Robert I's mother and daughter
both bore the name. Pet forms include Madge, Maidie,
Maisie. Also spelt Marjory, Margery. Marjory Fleming
(1803–11) was a child prodigy as a writer.

Mark, Marc

From Latin *martius*, 'warlike', which became Marcus. Also
a Biblical name, one of the Apostles. The two forms
combined put it into the top twenty for boys in 1996.

Martin

From Latin *martius*, 'warlike', but its medieval popularity
stems from St Martin of Tours. Pet forms are Mart, Marty.
Martin Martin (died 1719) was author of a famous
description of the Hebrides.

*Mary, Mhairi, Marie

From Hebrew, meaning 'the wished-for child'. Its older
Hebrew form was Miriam. Given special sanctity as the
name of the mother of Jesus, it has always been a very
popular name in Scotland, in English, French and Gaelic
forms, although in latter years its use has declined.
Scotland's only two ruling queens were both called Mary.
Pet forms include Molly, Polly, Minnie, Mamie. The French
form, Marie, is also in regular use. Mary Garden (1874–
1967) was a famous Scottish opera singer.

Matthew

From Hebrew Mattathiah, 'gift of God'. The name of one
of the Twelve Apostles, it has never gone quite out of

favour since the Middle Ages. It is currently very popular. Pet forms are Matt, Matty. Sir Matt Busby (1909–96) was a celebrated football manager.

Maureen
From Gaelic Mairin, a pet form of Mhairi, the Gaelic form of Mary.

*Mavis
From the bird name. The mavis is the song thrush.

Meg *see* Margaret.

Megan
A Welsh diminutive of Margaret, which has caught on in Scotland at the expense of other forms of this traditionally Scottish name; it is one of the top ten.

Melissa
From a Greek root meaning 'honeybee'. It is a popular name today and is one of the top fifty girls' names.

Mhairi *see* Mary.

Michael
From Hebrew, 'who is like God', the name of one of the three angels mentioned in the Bible. Always a frequently used name. Pet forms are Mike, Micky. The *Great Michael* was an early Scottish warship, and the scholar Michael Scott (*c*.1175–*c*.1230) also had a formidable reputation as a wizard.

Minnie *see* **Mary.**

Miriam *see* **Mary.**

*Mitchell
A surname form of Michael that is also given as a boy's
first name. The pet form is Mitch.

Mohammed
The name of the prophet of Islam and its prevalence is a
sign of the development of Scotland's Islamic community.
In 1996 this became the 100th most common first name.

Moira
There is an Irish place and earldom of this name, although
the personal name is an anglicised form of Maureen.

Molly *see* **Mary.**

*Morag
The Gaelic form of Sarah.

*Morven
A Celtic girl's name related to Cornish Morwenna,
although there is a mountain on the Caithness-Sutherland
border of the same name, from Gaelic *mor bheinn*, 'great
hill'. The mountainous peninsula southwest of Fort
William in the Highlands is called Morvern.

*Mungo
From Old Gaelic, meaning 'dear one'. Another name for
Kentigern, one of the great Celtic saints and specially

associated with Glasgow. Mungo Park (1771–1806) was a famous explorer of Africa.

*Munro

Surname of the Easter Ross clan, perhaps from Old Gaelic *mon ruadh*, 'red hill'. It is sometimes used as a first name.

*Murdo, Murdoch

From Gaelic *murchaidh*, 'sea warrior'. A name most usually found in the northwest and the Hebrides and currently rare.

*Muriel

From Old Gaelic *murgheal*, 'sea-bright'. Muriel Spark (born 1918) is perhaps Scotland's finest modern novelist.

*Murray

From the surname Murray, a form of Moray, from Old Gaelic words meaning 'at the edge of the sea'.

N

Nancy
A pet form both of Ann and of Agnes but with a long
history as a name in its own right. Not currently in favour.

Natalie
From Latin root words meaning 'born at Christmas',
although it is by no means restricted to people born on 25
December.

Natasha
A Russian form of Natalie, perhaps also confused with
Anastasia, which is also a popular Russian name, although
from Greek, meaning 'resurrected'. Both Natasha and
Natalie are equally popular names.

Neal, Neale *see* Neil.

*Nectan
An ancient royal name of Pictish origin; the root *nig* means
'to wash', hence 'purified one'. Nectansmere in Angus is
the site of a battle between Picts and Angles from
Northumbria.

*Neil, Niall
From Irish Gaelic Nia, 'champion', and appears in Norse as

Njal. The Norman French form was Nesle, from which came Nigel on the mistaken assumption that it came from Latin *niger*, 'black'. A name from Celtic legend, with the tale of Niall of the Nine Hostages, an early fifth-century Irish king. Alternative forms include Neal, Neale, Neill. Neil Gunn (1891–1973) was a major Scottish novelist.

Nell, Nella, Nellie *see* Helen.

Niall *see* Neil.

Nicholas
From Greek root words meaning 'victory of the people'. St Nicholas of Myra was the prototype of Santa Claus. It is not nearly so common with boys as Nicole is with girls, but it is still in the top hundred.

*Nicol, Nicoll
These are forms of Nicholas, and it is also a surname.

Nicole, Nicola
The French and Italian feminine forms of Nicholas. Nicola is a name often given at present when the fashion is mainly for French forms, as with Sophie, Louise, etc, but Nicola is not far behind. Together they make the sixth most popular girl's name of 1996.

Nicoll *see* Nicol.

Nigel
From the Latinised form of Neil, Nigellus. *See* Neil.

*Ninian

From the Old Gaelic personal name Ninidh, in modern Gaelic, Ringean. St Ninian, one of the fathers of the Celtic Church, founded a famous monastery at Whithorn in the fifth century.

*Norrie

From the surname, from Scandinavian Norge, Norway, indicating a northlander. The name may also be a pet form of Norman, although the ultimate source is very similar.

Norman

From Old English and Scots 'north man', a Viking. It was a popular name with the MacLeods.

*Norval

A name thought to have been invented by James Macpherson in his verse romance 'Ossian' but also an old surname, a shortened form of Normanville, occurring from the fourteenth century.

O

Oonagh *see* **Una**.

*Ossian ✓
From Gaelic *oisean*, 'little deer'. A rare name, although made famous by the 'Ossian' poems, supposedly translated from Gaelic by James Macpherson in the eighteenth century. Ossian was the legendary Gaelic bard and warrior, son of Fingal.

P

Paddy *see* **Patrick.**

Paige
A recently favoured girl's name, still climbing in popularity.

Patricia
The feminine form of Patrick, once popular but currently out of fashion. Pet forms are Pat, Patsy, Trish, Trisha. The form Tricia is also found as a name in its own right.

*Patrick
From Latin *patricius*, 'of noble birth'; Padraig in Gaelic. St Patrick, who converted the Irish to Christianity, is said to have been born in the west of Scotland. For a long time, and up to the nineteenth century, Peter (Gaelic Pedair) and Patrick were interchangeable. Thus Neil Munro's popular character Peter MacFarlane was nicknamed Para (Patrick) Handy. Despite Patrick's great popularity in Ireland, it was introduced there from Scotland. The pet form is Pat, the forms Paddy and Patsy being almost exclusively Irish. Sir Patrick Manson (1844–1922) is known as 'the father of tropical medicine'.

Patsy *see* **Patricia, Patrick.**

Paul
From Latin Paulus, 'little': a Biblical name from St Paul (whose Hebrew name was Saul), the first coordinator of the early Church.

Peggy
A pet form of Margaret.

Peter
From Greek *petros*, 'rock'. 'On this rock I will found my Church,' said Christ of his disciple Simon Peter. A popular name in medieval times and very much in current use. The pet form is Pete. *See also* Patrick.

Polly
A pet form of Mary now used as a name in its own right.

Q

Quentin
From Latin *quintus*, 'fifth'. Perhaps originally applied to a fifth child in times of regular births and high infant mortality, but it was a common Roman first name. Once much used in Scotland but now rare. Quentin Kennedy (1520–64) was an opponent of the Reformers.

R

*Rab, Rabbie

Shortened forms of Robert, more often found as Rab than
Rabbie. In both cases, a tribute to the immortal memory of
Robert Burns, with in recent years a nod also to the
popular comic character Rab C. Nesbitt portrayed on
television by Greg Fisher.

Rachel, Rachael

From Hebrew, meaning 'ewe' or 'ewe lamb'. A very
popular name in both forms, with Rachel preferred. Rachel
Carson (1907–64) was a prominent conservationist.

*Rae

A boy's or girl's name. Originally a surname, perhaps from
Gaelic *rath*, 'grace'.

*Ramsay

Originally a surname. James Ramsay Macdonald (1866–
1937), always known as Ramsay, was the first Labour
prime minister of Britain.

*Ranald

A form of Reginald, from Scandinavian *rognvaldr*, 'power in
counsel'. *See also* Ronald. The pet form is Ran.

Rebecca
From Hebrew, 'fair to look upon'. A Biblical name;
Rebecca was wife to Isaac and mother of Jacob and Esau.
Of limited usage in the past, it has become highly popular
and has been in the top ten girls' names in recent years.
The form Rebekah is also used. Pet forms are Becky, Becca.

Reece, Rhys
A Welsh name for boys whose use in Scotland, especially
as Reece, is increasing.

*Reid
A surname that is also found as a first name. From Middle
English and Scots *reed*, 'red', and often an English form of
Gaelic *ruadh*, 'red'. As with other names that were
originally nicknames, the colour association is long
forgotten.

*Rhona, Rona
This may be a feminine form of Ronan (from Gaelic *ron*,
'little seal') or from the island name (from Scandinavian
hraun-ey, 'rough island'). But as St Ronan lived and died on
North Rona, the two names are in any case intertwined.

Rob *see* Robert.

Robbie
This pet form of Robert is increasing rapidly in use as a
name in its own right.

Robert
From the Old Germanic elements *hrothi*, 'fame', and

berhta, 'bright', a warrior's name. A popular name since the time of King Robert I, the Bruce (1274–1329), it still appears in the top fifty boys' names. Pet forms include Bob, Bobby, Rob, Robbie, Robin. Notable Roberts include a regicide (of King James I), Sir Robert Graham, as well as the poets Fergusson and Burns, and the architect Robert Adam.

Robin
A pet form of Robert (Burns often referred to himself as Robin) but long in use as a name in its own right. There is a girl's form also, usually spelt Robyn. Robina is rarer.

*Roderick
From Gaelic *ruadh-ri*, 'red king'. An ancient name, borne in its Welsh form, Rhydderch, by a sixth-century king of Strathclyde. Pet forms include Rod, Roddie, Rory.

Ron *see* Ronald.

Rona *see* Rhona.

*Ronald
Scottish version, with Ranald, of the English Reginald, from Scandinavian *rognvaldr*, 'power in counsel'. Pet forms are Ron, Ronnie. Sir Ronald Ross (1857–1932) discovered the cause of malaria. Ronnie Corbett, the actor, was born in Edinburgh.

*Ronan
From Irish Gaelic *ron*, 'little seal'. This was the name of a number of saints of the Celtic Church. *See also* Rhona.

*Rory

A pet form of Roderick (Gaelic Ruairidh) but also used as a name in its own right.

*Ross

From Celtic *ros*, 'a promontory'; a surname associated with the far north and also the southwest. In recent years it has become a very popular first name and is in the top ten boys' names.

*Rowan

An unusual name, and used in equal numbers for boys and girls, from the tree, Gaelic *ruadhan*, 'little red one', a popular feature of the Scottish countryside with its bright red berries.

*Roy

From Gaelic *ruadh*, 'red'; also from Old French *roy*, 'king'.

*Ryan

Originally an Irish surname, from an Old Celtic word meaning 'chief' although there is also a Loch Ryan in southwest Scotland. This has become an extremely popular boy's name, number one in 1996, influenced perhaps by the American film star Ryan O'Neal.

S

Sal, Sally
Pet forms of Sarah, with Sally, in particular, often used as a name in its own right.

Sam, Samuel
As with many other long-established names, the pet form of Samuel is now used more often as a name than is the original. From Hebrew root words meaning 'heard by God', Samuel was the name of one of the great Biblical prophets. The other pet form is Sammy. Samuel Colt (1814–62), inventor of the revolving pistol, was of Scots descent. As a girl's name, Sam is the pet form of Samantha.

Samantha
A name that became immensely popular in the 1980s and is still in the top twenty. The American television series *Bewitched*, with a character of this name, helped its rise. The pet form is Sam.

Samuel *see* Sam.

Sanders
A shortened form of Alexander, in use as a surname (also found as Saunders) and occasionally found as a first name, especially in the north.

*Sandra
A shortened form of Alexandra, in common use as a name in its own right as a feminine equivalent of Sanders.

*Sandy
Shortened form of Alexander. Once this name could be used as a synonym for a male Scot, along with Jock. It seems to be making a modest comeback as a name in its own right.

Sarah
From the Hebrew word for a 'princess'. A Biblical name; Sarah was wife to Abraham and mother of Isaac. A very popular name in modern times, in the top ten for girls. Its Gaelic equivalent is the dissimilar-sounding Morag. Pet forms are Sal, Sally.

Saunders *see* Sanders.

*Scott
The surname of a border clan and in recent years one of the most often used first names for boys, perhaps stimulated in the later twentieth century by television's *Star Trek*, but also as a patriotic gesture. Scottie is a pet form. Scott Hastings is one of Scottish rugby's star international players.

Sean, Shaun
Irish Gaelic form of John, and more common now in Scotland than Iain. The Scottish film star Sean Connery contributed to its popularity.

*Seonaid, Shona

Gaelic and Scots forms of Irish Gaelic Sinead, Janet.
Sinead itself, helped by performers like Sinead Cusack, is
highly popular.

Seumas *see* Hamish.

Shannon

Another Irish name for girls that has recently appeared. It
is now strongly established and was fourth in popularity in
1996.

Shaun *see* Sean.

Sheana *see* Sheena.

*Sheila

A variant form of Irish Gaelic Sile, Celia. The Australian
equivalent of Bruce for girls. The form Sheilagh, once
popular, is now outmoded.

*Sheena, Sheana

From Irish Gaelic Sine, Janet or Jane. *See also* Seonaid.

Shona *see* Seonaid.

Simon

From a Hebrew root meaning 'listening'. It is a Biblical
name much used in Scotland. It is particularly associated
with the Lovat Frasers, so many of whose chiefs were
called Simon that they were known as MacShimi. The
French form Simone is often found as a girl's name. Pet
forms, uncommon nowadays, are Sim, Simmie.

*Sinclair

From French Saint Clair, a surname that has become a first name.

Sinead *see* Seonaid.

*Somerled

From Old Norse Sumarlioi, 'summer wanderer'. The name of the earliest Lord of the Isles, founder of Clans MacDonald and MacDougall. *See also* Sorley (below) and Somhairle (Gaelic names, page 95).

Sophie

From Greek *sophia*, 'divine wisdom'. Sophia was the typical form in past times but it is now rare; however, as Sophie, it is one of the top twenty girls' names today.

*Sorley

An English-language variant of Somerled. Sorley Maclean (1911–96) was one of the great Gaelic poets of the twentieth century.

Stephanie

Feminine form of French Stephane, Stephen, and a consistently popular girl's name in recent years.

Steven, Stephen

From Greek *stephanos*, 'garlanded'. St Stephen was the first Christian martyr and helped to give the name popularity in the Middle Ages. The Steven form is more usual in Scotland than Stephen. Pet forms are Steve, Stevie, Steenie. Stephen Hendry became the youngest world snooker champion.

Stewart *see* **Stuart.**

*Struan
Territorial name from Struan in Perthshire, a boy's name associated especially with the Robertsons.

*Stuart, Stewart
In medieval Scotland, the steward was a high official, deputy to the king in most things, and often related to the royal house. With Robert II, the Stewards or Stewarts became the Scottish royal house and eventually a clan with several locations. The French form Stuart became current during the sixteenth century with the close political association between Scotland and France. Both forms are used, the Stewart one more often when there is a direct family link with the name. The pet form is Stu.

T

*Tam

Once used only as a Scots pet form of Thomas, now sometimes used in its own right. Tam Dalyell MP is named after his ancestor, the royalist General Tam Dalyell (c.1615–85).

Tammas *see* Thomas.

*Tammy

The current form of Thomasina, which is now outmoded. Tamsin is also found but is more rare.

Taylor

Steadily climbing in popularity as a girl's name although still unusual.

Tearlach *see* Charles.

Thomas

From an Aramaic root, meaning 'twin'; the name of one of the Apostles. It was an extremely popular name in the Middle Ages, as can be seen from the number of Thomsons to be found in Scotland. Pet forms include Tam, Tammas, Tom, Tommy. Thomas Hope (1766–1844) was a pioneer of modern chemistry. Tommy Docherty was one of Scotland's many great footballers.

Thomasina
A feminine form of Thomas. *See* Tammy.

Tina *see* Catriona.

Tom, Tommy *see* Thomas.

*Torquil
Gaelic Torcuill, from Old Norse Thorketil, 'kettle or vessel of Thor', the god of thunder. A popular name with the MacLeods, Nicolsons and other clans of the northwest.

Tricia
A pet form of Patricia that is also used as a name in its own right.

Trina *see* Catriona.

Trish, Trisha *see* Patricia.

u

*Una

Una is Latin for 'one', but the name comes from Irish Gaelic Oonagh. The name features in Spenser's sixteenth-century English poem *The Faerie Queen*, which was read and admired in Scotland.

V

Veronica

From Greek/Latin roots meaning 'true image'. St Veronica cleansed the face of Christ on the road to Calvary. Found in Scotland from the seventeenth century, the shortened form Vera (Latin *vera*, 'true') is also a name in its own right.

W

*Wallace

From a Celtic name indicating a Briton of Strathclyde who spoke a language similar to Welsh. The surname of Sir William Wallace, the great defender of Scotland's independence (*c.*1274–1305), it has become a first name in modern times. Also spelt Wallas. The name Wally, which has become derogatory, is probably from Oliver.

Walter

From Old Germanic *wealdhere*, 'strong warrior'. In frequent use in Scotland from the twelfth century, it has given rise to common surnames like Watt, Watson and Waterston. It is currently rare. Pet forms include Wat, Wattie. Sir Walter Scott (1771–1832), novelist and poet, is perhaps the most famous bearer of the name.

Wendy

A name invented by the Scots writer, Sir J. M Barrie, author of *Peter Pan* (1904), in which Wendy is a character. It quite soon came into use as a first name and remains popular. Wendy Wood was a doughty campaigner for Scottish independence.

*Willa

Feminine form of Will, itself a shortened version of

William. Willa Muir (1890–1970) was a gifted writer and translator.

William
From Old Germanic Wilihelm, 'helmet of resolution', and brought to Scotland by twelfth-century Norman settlers. The name of an early Scottish king, William the Lion, and of William Wallace, it has always been a popular choice in Scotland. Although overtaken by Liam, it remains in the top fifty. Pet forms are Willie, Will, Billy, Bill. Willie Carson was the first Scotsman to be champion jockey.

Gaelic First Names

Further details about individual names are given under the English forms.

The pronunciation guide can only be approximate.

Aindrea (An-dra): Andrew, 'manly'.

Alasdair (Alister): Alexander, 'defender of men'.

Aonghas (Eun-eu-uss): Angus, 'the unique choice".

Artair (Ar-tur): Arthur, 'bear-like'.

Cailean (Cal-yan): Colin, 'child'.

Calum (Cal-lum): Colm, Malcolm, 'dove'.

Catriona (Ca-treeona): Catherine, 'pure one'.

Ciaran (Kee-ran): 'dark one'.

Coinneach (Kon-yach): Kenneth, 'the fair one'.

Deórsa (Jee-orsa): George, 'farmer'. *See also* Seóras'.

Domhnall (Daw-ull): Donald, 'the great chief'.

Donnchadh (Don-a-chaw): Duncan, 'brown warrior'.

Dùghall (Doo-wall):Dougal, 'dark stranger'.

Eachann (Ya-chun): Hector, 'steadfast'.

Ealasaid (Yall-a-sutch): Elizabeth, 'dedicated to God'.

Eilidh (Ay-lee): Helen, 'light'.

Eoghan (Yo-wun): Ewan, 'dedicated to the yew tree'.

Fearchar (Fer-a-char): Farquhar, 'very dearest one'.

Fearghas (Fair-a-chas): Fergus, 'super choice'.

Fionnaghal (Fyon-a-hal): Fenella, 'white-shoulders'.

Fionnlagh (Fyon-a-low): Finlay, 'fair hero'.

Gilleasbuig (Gheel-yes-pic): Gillespie, 'servant of the bishop'.

Giorsail (Ghee-orsal): 'grace'.

Iomhair (Ee-eu-var): Ivar, 'archer'.

Iseabail (Eesh-a-bal): Isabel, 'dedicated to God'.

Lachlann (Lach-lunn): Lachlan, 'Norseman'.

Lúthais (Loo-ass): Lewis, 'famous warrior'.

Maili (Ma-lee): Molly, May, 'pearl'.

Mairead (Ma-ee-rat): Mary.

Mairearad (Ma-ee-rye-rat): Margaret, 'pearl'.

Marsaili (Mar-sally): Marjorie, 'pearl'.

Mhairi (Va-ree): Mary, 'longed-for child'.

Mórag (Mo-rac): Morag, Sarah, 'princess'.

Murchadh (Moor-a-chaw): Murdo, 'sea-fighter'.

Niall (Nyee-ull): Neil, 'champion'.

Pádraig (Paw-dreek): Patrick, 'noble one'.

Peadar (Pay-dur): Peter, 'rock'.

Raghnall (Ren-ull): Ronald, 'wise power'.

Ruairidh (Ro-arree): Roderick, 'famous ruler'.

Seonag (Shaw-nuck): Joan, 'gift of God'.

Seonaid (Shaw-nutch): Janet, 'gift of God'.

Seóras (Shaw-russ): George, 'farmer'.

Seumas (Shay-muss): James, 'the supplanter'.

Sìleas (Shee-luss): Julia, 'youth'.

Sìm (Sheem): Simon, 'the listener'.

Sìne (Shee-nuh): Jane, Jean, 'gift of God'.

Siobhán (Shee-vawn): Judith, 'Jewish one'.

Siusaidh (Shoo-see): Susan, 'lily'.

Somhairle (Sorr-lee): Sorley, Somerled, 'summer wanderer'.

Tearlach (Tchar-lach): Charles, 'manly'.

Torcuill (Torr-kooil): Torquil, 'Thor's kettle'.

Tormod (Torr-o-mot): Norman, 'northman'.

Uilleam (Ool-yam): William, 'strong helmet'.

Uisdean (Oosh-tyan): Hugh, 'spiritual one'.

Una (Oo-na): Winifred, 'white wave'.

Acknowledgement

The most comprehensive source on the use of first names in Scotland is the General Register Office in Edinburgh which publishes a useful booklet, *Personal Names in Scotland*, obtainable on request for a small fee, and which records all new names with an annual report.